STORY STREET

SANDRA HENEFIELD

WESTBOW
PRESS®
A DIVISION OF THOMAS NELSON
& ZONDERVAN

THE HOLY BIBLE, NEW INTERNATIONAL VERSION®,
NIV® Copyright © 1973, 1978, 1984, 2011 by Biblica, Inc.®
Used by permission. All rights reserved worldwide.

Scripture taken from the King James Version of the Bible.

WestBow Press books may be ordered through booksellers or by contacting:

WestBow Press
A Division of Thomas Nelson & Zondervan
1663 Liberty Drive
Bloomington, IN 47403
www.westbowpress.com
1 (866) 928-1240

ISBN: 978-1-9736-4375-3 (sc)
ISBN: 978-1-9736-4376-0 (hc)
ISBN: 978-1-9736-4374-6 (e)

Library of Congress Control Number: 2018912785

Print information available on the last page.

WestBow Press rev. date: 10/25/2018

Dedicated to Cole Depriest

Cole loved life and lived it to the fullest. He played baseball with the Carthage Dixie League and enjoyed swimming, hunting, and working on the ranch. He especially enjoyed rodeoing and was a member of PYRA, East Texas Equestrian Drill Team, and SCSP Association. He earned 2014 SCSP (six and under) All-Around Champion award. Cole was a special little cowboy who never met a stranger. He had that special spark that made everyone love him. He always wore a smile as wide as the Sabine River and a grin that could melt an iceberg. At only eight, he could do more than many adults. Thanks to his infectious personality, it only took a few minutes to fall in love with him. Every person who knew Cole is better for it. Cole seemed to live life in the fast lane, as if he couldn't get it done quickly enough, as if he knew his time here was limited. He was called home too soon, yet was far too special to stay long on earth. God blessed his family and friends by sending an angel to earth, even if it were for just a short space of time.

Acknowledgment

Gracie Kinney and Wesley Kinney for editing and technical support.

The Village and the Vessels

In the beginning, there was an island surrounded by a beautiful, crystal-like sea. The turquoise-blue sky was reflected like a mirror by the color of the water covering the coral reef that lay beneath the waves.

The bright, orange sun warmed the island and the waters by day. The perfect, round moon, hanging on nothing in the sky, would light the land below as the island people rested.

The white, foamy waves would crash against the seashore. The sound brought peace and a sense that all was calm, like music made only by waves and wind.

When the sun rose, it sent the moon on its way for the day to dawn. The island came alive to the sounds of children running and playing on the seashore. They would be laughing and playing tag with their toes as the cool ocean would catch them at the edge of the seashore.

The seagulls would sing and sweep over the ocean, looking for food. This was the way the Creator meant things to be. As he would sit, watching from above, using the island as his footstool, he was at rest, thinking, *What I made is good!*

I had read and dreamed about this island. I wanted to visit

and imagine what a village like this would be. My adventure started as I arrived by a dream on the beautiful seashore, where I watched the children laugh and play. As a child, I had too much energy. I was even happy with them for a little while as we danced in the waves together, and no one was telling me to calm down. As I turned, I could see a path leading away from the ocean, and I headed that way. Hopefully, it would lead me to the village I had dreamed of.

As I walked along, the sand turned to more solid ground, and beautiful, tall green trees shot up around me. Fragrant flowers of beautiful colors, like those of a rainbow, were everywhere to behold. There was so much to take in, so I slowed my search for the village just to worship the Creator of all of this.

I was startled by a big black bear that paid me no attention. A large lizard just kept moving on. Many other animals passed in front of me, and even a deer decided to walk alongside me. I am sure the deer was panting for fresh water, as deer do daily. I had heard that the Creator lived among the village people. He had even named the village people "vessels" and had written each of their names in a book of life after he created them with his own hands.

My path came to a wooden bridge. As I crossed over, I stopped to look at the fish swimming below and the birds perched on the railings. I did not seem to bother them, and being a lover of bird watching, I stopped and gazed at them. Red birds, yellow finches, and even bluebirds that do not like other birds were there.

The path began to grow wider now, and I could hear the

sound of the village people scurrying around. The sweet smell of morning pastries with cinnamon and sugar lingered in the air. Scents of fresh bread also caused me to sense how hungry I was. But I was hungrier to find the Creator than to feed myself at this time.

I finally made it to the village, and it was beautiful, with cobblestone roads. There were many vessels smiling and talking to one another. They seemed to care for each other. I also noticed some who had sadness on their faces and probably grief in their hearts. But I smiled at everyone and just kept on looking for the Creator. I heard he had a workshop here and welcomed all who came to spend time with him. It seemed his time was endless for those who wanted to visit with him.

I noticed a little blind boy vessel with a cane, moving along. He had on dark glasses, but it seemed he did not smile. And then there was a little girl vessel talking excessively to a little boy vessel sitting on a curb as he shook his head. Through a window, I saw a lady vessel teaching a little girl vessel how to play the piano.

I also saw a little blonde-haired girl vessel kneeling down at the candy store, looking at the sweet-smelling pink gum. "Do not touch," the mom vessel seemed to say. But the best was a little boy vessel with a smile so big, dressed up like a cowboy. He had a big hat and boots and was roping everything he could as he walked down the street.

I must be getting close to the shop of the Creator, I thought. But there was a strange sight: an old lady vessel was peeking at me from behind a curtain. I wondered what the fence was all about. She was scary. *Oh, me! I must keep going.*

And then I saw an unusual building in the distance. Was that it? There was a beautiful, flowing fountain in front of it, where the water seemed to change as colors of the rainbow. *This must be it,* I thought, as behind the fountain, I could see a marble building. It had a sign that simply said, "Creator." I had found him, and I ran with joy!

I stood reverently at the door and knocked quietly. Immediately, a strong, kind voice said, "Come in." An olive-skinned man was sitting behind a potter's wheel, quietly working with his hands. He would scoop up water from a wooden bucket, mix it with a pile of sand, and make clay. Then he would mold it with his hands ever so carefully.

I was speechless, and as someone who never stopped talking, I knew I was in the presence of something amazing. After a few moments, the Creator stopped the wheel and simply said, "Are you hungry?"

I was thinking he was going to offer me some of those amazing pastries or fresh bread that I had smelled coming into the village. I said, "Yes, I am."

Instead, he offered me blackened fish and some very flat bread with a cup of water. I must admit, it was the best fish I had ever eaten, and the bread was good also. The water was almost sweet and so cold, and it tasted so good. He must have gotten the water from a very deep well.

While we were eating together, I could not stop smiling at him. He nicely said, after I apologized for smiling, "I made you that way." Wow, being in his presence made me feel so much better.

"Thanks," I said. "I get into a lot of trouble for talking too much and having too much energy."

"Oh, I know," he kindly said. "Remember—I made you. You have sometimes have brought me honor, and other times, you have brought me dishonor, but I love you either way. My love has no limits or boundaries. I created you with your own will. I love you, my vessel," he said to me. "I know you know I redeemed you with my own blood. You belong to me, and today, you returned to me for this visit. I love when my vessels come to spend time with me. My time is endless to spend with them."

As he finished eating, he said, "Sit here a while, and watch me create a new vessel for the village. But we can talk some as I work. I can do a lot of things at the same time," the Creator said with a smile.

He darkened the room without a voice, and a light shone over the potter's wheel as he began to spin it with his own hands. With his own hands, be began to shape and bring a new vessel for the village to life. As he spun the wheel, mixing the clay and water, the vessel began to take a shape. As he spoke, he told me that no two vessels he had ever made were the same. They might be similar, since they all have one Creator, but each vessel was unique, with its own purpose and plan to live out in the village among other vessels.

As he spun the wheel, he looked deep into my eyes as into my soul and said, "I know you have had some pain, shame, and great sorrow in your life—some pain, shame, and sorrow you caused from your choices and sin. And then other vessels brought some pain, shame, and sorrow upon you. But I am proud of you, as you have sought my forgiveness and healing. You also have asked forgiveness from other vessels that you have hurt along your way. Continue to be a vessel of love to others, and I will be watching and encouraging you along to fulfill your purpose and plan. I am glad you came to visit and have a meal with me. This so pleases me."

Our visit was coming to a close this day, but I could not contain myself as I stood and asked if I could hug him. He extended grace and mercy to me with the biggest and tightest hug I had ever received. The love of the Creator was pure.

As I turned to walk out the door, I told him that I had been writing for many years about the vessels I had met on my journey. "I want to tell their stories of your love and grace that you gave them."

He said, "I know that you have encountered many of my vessels. Tell their stories, and tell how I created each with a purpose and a plan. And continue to tell them that I sent my only son Jesus to die for sins, to be buried, and to rise from the dead. Tell them to follow me and listen to my voice. Tell them that I long for them to return to me, their Creator, one day and be completely redeemed and live with me."

Too Much Energy

First-grade Sandy was the shortest girl in her class. She had red hair and freckles. People made fun of her and made her upset. She wasn't mean to other kids—she tried hard to be friendly. But she had a big problem that made it tough for people to like her.

Sandy had trouble controlling herself. She talked way too much, and she couldn't sit still. One time, she turned her desk over just by rocking it back and forth. All the kids laughed out loud, but the teacher didn't; she just shook her head sadly at Sandy.

Then there was the time the teacher was out of the classroom and Sandy turned her desk upside down and made a slide out of it. When the teacher came back to the room, she took Sandy to the principal's office. They called her mom to come and get her. Sandy tried hard to be good and sit still, but it didn't work. She had too much energy.

Sandy wasn't dumb. In fact, she finished her schoolwork before everyone else and made a hundred on her tests. But all that energy and creativity got her into trouble. Her mom cried a lot. Her dad tried to make her be still. Even though they loved her very much, that didn't solve her problem.

It was a good thing Sandy had a big God to help her! Sandy believed in Jesus as her Savior and she knew God loved her. She heard it from her mom and dad all the time, and even at church, she would hear of how God loved her so much. She was thankful for that because she wondered how anyone could love someone who was always in trouble. Sandy loved God so much, but people just thought she was bad because she was so noisy and hyperactive.

Sandy learned that God answers prayer. So she began to ask God to help her be still and not talk so much. She would quote the verse, "Be still and know that I am God," over and over.

Her dad had built her a giant swing set. He made it so she

couldn't flip it over from swinging too high. She went there to use up her energy. And she went there to pray and sing because she knew God was watching her and listening to her. "Help me, God, please," she prayed. "You made me, and you can help me!"

In second grade, Sandy moved to a new city and a new school. She was determined to sit still and not talk. She decided to keep very busy in school. Wanting to please her new teacher, she took her brand-new math workbook home and finished it in one weekend. It was supposed to have lasted for the whole year. She got in major trouble for that. It seemed trouble was everywhere for her even in doing good. Her energy was too much for everyone. She continued to ask God for help.

Sandy kept praying, and soon the Holy Spirit began to work in her life. She could tell He was changing her. She could sit still and stay quiet longer. God was helping her have self-control.

At Christmas, when school was almost out for the holidays, the teacher asked Sandy to take home the class parakeet. She couldn't believe it. The teacher said, "You have been so good the last few weeks!" Sandy knew it was God helping her. Self-control was becoming part of her life. God was real to her, and she began to pray even more.

God had given Sandy all her energy. As Sandy grew up, she found she could use it to do lots of things: to sing, play piano and other instruments, and of course, talk. She still talks too much, but she has found out God had a plan for using that talent too. God took Sandy's greatest weakness—talking too much—and made it her greatest strength. Today, she talks to kids about Jesus wherever she is. She may be teaching piano or voice, but she always talks about Jesus her Savior and how He can help you in life. She talks to anyone who will listen about her favorite person Jesus and the God who is real to her.

She still has too much energy, but God helps her daily to use it for Him. She starts every morning out asking God to help her use her life and words to honor Him.

He is a big God who made her just right, and now, as she teaches kids all over, she understands those who cannot sit still or be quiet.

God sees your heart and knows if you love Him! Remember—God answers the prayers of His children. Pray and believe God will help you. He'll be there for you the same way He is for Sandy!

The Sweet Temptation

Dad had left for work, and this was the morning every week the three little girls, Gracie, Mackenzie and Chloe, went grocery shopping with Mom. Mom always let them pick out one favorite treat at the store. They knew the routine of holding on to the basket, except for Chloe, who still got to ride in the buggies.

They each had to wait patiently till they got to the aisle where their favorite treat was. The girls, though they were close in age and looked alike, had very different taste in their treats. Gracie, the oldest, loved chocolate cupcakes with filling in the middle. Mackenzie loved red jelly rolls with sweet sugar icing on them. And then there was Chloe, who loved olives and pickles and anything salty. One time, Chloe ate a whole jar of olives without getting sick! Yes, God in His designing them had made three unique little blonde-headed girls with different tastes and likes.

Every week as they headed for the checkout counter, they held their special treats as if they were gold. The basket was overflowing with good food to fill the pantry and refrigerator, and they were so thankful. Mom always reminded them of how good God was in providing for them, and also how they needed to share some of this food with others. Then the girls always picked out some special treat for their dad.

As the basket sat next to the checkout counter, there it was: "the sweet temptation"! The sweet smell of sugar lingered in the air around the candy and gum counter. It was placed right at eye level for short little children. The girls always asked for more treats as they looked at the counter, but Mom would say, "No, girls, you picked out your treats." Week after week, "the sweet temptation" was there at the checkout.

Then one week, it happened. Mackenzie could not resist any longer. When no one was looking, she slipped a piece of gum, the sweet temptation, into her hand. As they continued to check out, she thought how sweet this pink gum would taste later. Mackenzie closed her hand tightly to hide it from her mom. She thought, *I'll go to my room and close the door and eat it, and no one will know.* Mackenzie forgot that God, who loves her, sees all things.

Upon leaving the store, her mother noticed that Mackenzie was very quiet. While loading the groceries into the car, Mother saw Mackenzie's hand closed tight. She asks Mackenzie to show her what was in her hand. Slowly, she opened her hand and looked up at her mom. "What have you done?" Mom said sadly. Mackenzie looked down, knowing she had been caught. Her mom said, "Well, you will have to take the gum back into the store and tell the manager what you stole." Mackenzie could not believe her mom was going to make her take it back.

Mom quietly took all three girls back into the store. She then asked for the manager. When he came, Mackenzie had to give him the gum and say she was sorry. Mackenzie knew from God's word it was wrong to steal. The Bible says, "Do not steal!" This was something her dad and mom had taught her.

As they got back in the car, everyone was silent. Mom just said, "We'll talk about this when we get home." Mackenzie kept looking out the car window, wondering if the police were coming to get her. She knew bad people went to jail, and she had done something very bad.

Upon arriving home, her mom simply said, "Mackenzie, go to your room. I will be there in a little bit." This gave Mom some time to think and ask God for the wisdom to know what to say and do. As Mackenzie went down the hall, she was sad and worried about her punishment. She could not have her special treat yet either.

Mom opened the door, and there Mackenzie sat quietly on the bed. Mom sat next to her and said, "Mackenzie, what you did was wrong, and you know that, right?" Mackenzie nodded her head. Mom told her that she loved her and so did God. "You know, Mackenzie, this is why Jesus died. He died for our sins, the bad things we do and think. They nailed Jesus to a cross, and He died there on that cross. Jesus was God clothed in human form" (John 1:14). "It was Jesus's blood that paid for our sins. We pay for sweet candy and gum with money, but Jesus paid for our sins with His death. He did that for you, Mackenzie, because He loves you so much! God loves you, Mackenzie, so much. Do you believe that?" Mackenzie nodded her head. She felt so sorry and ashamed. Her mom continued, "And they buried Jesus in a tomb, and the Good News is, Mackenzie, He came back to life."

As Mackenzie looked up at her mother, she had tears in her eyes. "I am sorry He had to do that for me. I am sorry I stole the gum."

Mom said, "I also, MacKenzie, have done some bad things and thought some bad thoughts. But I have asked Jesus to forgive me, and He has, and I am going to heaven when I die. You can do that too."

"I can!" said Mackenzie.

Mom got her Bible and read John 3:16: "For God so loved the world that He gave His only begotten Son that whosoever believeth in Him (Jesus) should not perish but have everlasting life." That very day, Mackenzie trusted Jesus as her Savior and became one of God's forever children.

Mackenzie prayed and said, "I believe you died for me, Jesus, and I want to go to heaven with Mommy someday. Please forgive me, and thank you taking away all my sins! Amen."

Mom held Mackenzie so tightly, smiled, and said, "Let's go get that special treat, and can I have a bite?"

Mackenzie looked and sort of smiled at her mom and said, "Maybe a little bite, Mom!"

The Heart of Christmas

Meagan's favorite afternoon of the week had finally arrived! There was a chill in the air as she hurried to her piano lesson. Christmas was just a few weeks away, and she was excited because today she would get her new music book with Christmas songs in it. This would be her first year to play in the Christmas piano recital!

The colorful, twinkling Christmas lights were already showing up in places around town. Meagan loved thinking about her wish list and what would be under the tree that special morning. Yes, this was absolutely her favorite time of the year!

As she arrived, her redheaded piano teacher greeted her student at the door, smiling sweetly. Meagan sat down at the piano and saw her new book on the music stand. The colors on the outside were red, green, and white, with a beautiful Christmas tree on the front. Meagan was eager to learn the beautiful music of Christmas, but little did she know that what she was about to learn would change her life forever!

"Let's start with "Jingle Bells,"" said her teacher cheerfully. The song was fun and easy to learn. Meagan loved to imagine herself "dashing through the snow" as her fingers glided over the keys.

The next piece was "Away in a Manger." "Meagan, do you know what this song is about?" her teacher asked. The young student stared blankly at her teacher. Meagan had never been to church, and no one had ever shared with her what Christmas was really about. The teacher gently closed the piano book and had Meagan look at the front cover. "I'll give you a hint," she said with a twinkle in her eyes. "What is the title of this book?"

"*Christmas Favorites*," replied Meagan. Her teacher covered up the last part of the word *Christmas*. Meagan saw for the first time the name *Christ* in the word *Christmas*. A puzzled expression came over her face as she looked at her teacher.

"Who is Christ?" Meagan asked.

"Christ is the heart of Christmas," said her teacher with a

radiant smile on her face. Meagan was very puzzled now! Her teacher opened the piano book back to the song

"Away in a Manger" and began to tell the story of Jesus Christ.

Meagan sat in wonder and amazement! For the first time, the light of the gospel was opening her eyes to the Christ of Christmas. Her teacher had learned the story of the birth of Jesus as a little child, so she quoted the passage found in Luke2: 8–12 that she had memorized when she was nine years old.

"And there were shepherds living out in the fields nearby, keeping watch over their flocks at night. An angel of the Lord appeared to them, and the glory of the Lord shone around them, and they were terrified. But the angel said to them, "Do not be afraid. I bring you good news that will cause great joy for all the people. Today in the town of David a Savior has been born to you; He is the Messiah, the Lord. This will be a sign to you: You will find a baby wrapped in cloths and lying in a manger."

"So that's the baby I've seen sometimes at Christmas wrapped up in a blanket and lying on a bed of hay!" Meagan exclaimed.

"Yes," said her teacher with a smile. "The baby born was named Jesus, who is Christ the Lord. He was God's only Son, who came to earth as a little baby, lived a sinless life here on earth, and then died, just to be our Savior! He saved us from the punishment of our sins. Do you know what sin is?" asked her teacher.

Meagan thought about that and said, "Not really."

"God's words were written down for us in a book called the Bible. The Bible tells us that sin is disobeying God's laws, like lying or stealing, which God said we should not do. Have you ever lied or taken something that wasn't your?" her teacher asked.

Meagan replied softly, "Yes, sometimes I lie."

"Well, sad to say, I have too!" admitted her piano teacher. "The Bible calls that sin. I am not happy when I do that. God is sad when we sin because He created us and loves us very much, but He is perfectly holy. Sin separates us from being able to have a special relationship with God. That is why God sent Jesus to be our Savior."

Meagan still had a confused look on her face, so her teacher thought of another way to explain what she meant.

"If we went to the store this afternoon and I bought you an ice cream cone, I would pay for it with money, right?" Meagan nodded her head yes. "Well, Jesus Christ paid for your sin and mine with His death. Even though He had never sinned, He was nailed to an old wooden cross, just like a criminal. The Roman soldiers put a spear in His side, and His blood came out. It was a very painful for Him, but Jesus loved you and me so much that He did that for us. We should be punished for our sins, but there is nothing we could ever do that would be good enough to make things right. He took our place and paid that price in order for us to be forgiven and restore our relationship with God.

"Jesus took the punishment for all our sins, even the ones we haven't committed yet," her teacher continued, "so when we trust Jesus Christ as our Savior, we can be forgiven while we are here on earth, and then we can go to heaven when we die."

"There is another verse in the Bible that I love," said her teacher. "In the book of John, chapter 3, verse 16, it says, "For God so loved the world that He gave His one and only Son, that whoever believes in Him shall not perish but have eternal life."

"Heaven is a perfect place where sin, pain, and shame do not exist. Those who believe in Jesus and what He has done for them will be able to live eternally surrounded by His love and grace. Would you like to go there someday and be forever with Jesus?" her piano teacher asked kindly.

Meagan replied with a quiet and humble spirit, "Yes, I would. I want to trust Jesus as my Savior so I can go to heaven when I die." The teacher led Meagan in a quiet prayer, and right there, Meagan and her teacher thanked God for His forgiveness and His gift of eternal life.

From that moment on, Christmas would never be the same for Meagan. She finally understood the heart of Christmas! With a bright smile on her face, she looked up and said to her teacher, "Let's learn how to play 'Away in a Manger' right now!" And she did!

Today, will you receive the greatest gift of all? Simply trust in Jesus for the forgiveness of your sins and receive the gift of eternal life. He gives freely the gift of eternal life to anyone who believes.

"I write these things to you who believe in the name of the

Son of God so that you may know that you have eternal life" (1 John 5:13).

Jesus's name means "God our Savior, Keeper, and Defender!" Merry Christmas!

The Day Wrong Was Right

Clara woke up to the smell of pancakes cooking in the kitchen. The aroma of sweet syrup and hot butter melting made her want to get out of bed. Mornings were not her favorite time of the day. But her stomach was growling, and the smell of Mom's cooking made the sun coming up bearable. Clara did not want to talk or smile in the morning. Everyone needed to be quiet, so she thought. But with two little sisters and a dad who thought everyone should be gleeful in the morning, this did not make things easy for her. Sometimes, she had to go back to her room until she could be nice. Clara and her sisters ate their pancakes with peanut butter and syrup. It did not take her long to cheer up a little and come back quickly. She was afraid her sisters would eat her breakfast.

After her breakfast, Clara felt more like talking. When God created Clara in her mother's womb, God had given Clara a very smart, creative mind. She liked things neat and in order. She did not mind cleaning her room, which was all hers and had a pink-and-white-checkered bedspread and matching curtains. She knew about God and wanted to please Him and her parents. She spent much time with her mom, reading to her and helping her memorize Bible verses. She loved playing in her room alone and pretending she was reading books.

As I said, Clara had a very smart, creative mind. Her dad, every night after he had helped give the three little girls their bath, would sprinkle baby powder on them. It smelled so good and sweet, and he would say, "Now you are all clean, sweet girls!" Then he would play with them and read books and tuck them into bed. Clara loved the word *clean*—so we shall see.

One morning after her delicious breakfast, Mom told Clara "You need to go clean your room this morning. Make sure you do it well, so clean, clean, clean." So off Clara went down the hall and closed the door behind her. She so wanted to please her mom and God. She had been taught that Jesus is watching and wants us to always do our best. Clara got a creative idea about how to best clean her room.

The large baby powder container was sitting on the dresser from the night before after her bath. Her smart, creative mind thought, *Clean, clean—that's what baby powder does.* So Clara decided to use baby powder to clean, clean, clean the room. She put baby powder in between her sheets. *That smells good,* she thought. She put powder in the closet on the floor and even filled her shoes. She powdered the window seat and the floor, and in her mind, she had cleaned, cleaned, cleaned. *Mom is going to be so happy. Oh, let me put some in my drawers where my clothes are,* she sweetly thought. The whole large bottle of good-smelling baby powder was everywhere in the room. She was so proud! She could not wait for Mom to come and see.

Suddenly, Mom opened the door and thought the room was on fire. White smoke filled the air, and through the cloud, Clara was beaming with a big smile. "Clean, clean, clean!" she said with a big, sweet smile.

All of a sudden, she realized Mom was not smiling. Instead, Mom began to speak loudly and harshly to Clara. "What have you done, Clara?" She was gasping for air, and the baby powder looked like the room was full of white smoke. Mom was upset. "You cannot breathe in here. What have you done?" Mom said sternly.

Clara said, "I cleaned the room just like you said, clean, and clean, and baby powder cleans."

"Oh, my goodness, Clara," her mom said, and she was really mad at Clara. Mom's voice was not nice, and Clara could not understand what she had done wrong. So Mom scolded Clara for what she had done. Clara cried because in her mind she was doing right, but in her mom's mind, she had done wrong, wrong, wrong.

After Clara's mom began to clean up the room, Mom realized she was wrong in reacting like she had. Clara had done her best, and as a smart, creative child, Clara had done a childish thing, not a disobedient thing. Her mom heard a still, small voice saying, *She was just being creative and doing what she thought was cleaning. Besides, you tell her baby powder cleans. Oh me,* Mom said to herself and went looking for Clara in the other room. Clara was still upset and confused about what had just happened. Mom apologized to Clara for being so mad at her. Mom confessed to Clara, "Mommies sometimes make mistakes, and scolding you for this was wrong. I am so sorry, Clara. Can you forgive me? You were right, and I was wrong." Sweet, smart, creative-minded Clara came to her mom, and they held each other and gave each other a hug.

Mom had a big job now to clean, clean, clean! She sent Clara to play with her sisters in their room. By now, Mom was quietly laughing and thinking, *This will be a great story to tell their father when he gets home, no baby powder tonight! We are out!*

Blind to God's Love

The phone rang early one beautiful, sunny morning. The lady on the phone wanted her son to take piano lessons from me. She said that Wesley, her son, is blind but very smart. She was very persistent, so I told her I would try. I had been teaching for many years, but I never had taught a blind student how to play the piano. I was up for another adventure in learning.

As I opened the door the next day, there stood a very handsome, dark-haired young boy with a little cane and dark sunglasses. His mother Wendy introduced me, and from that moment on, I was taken by Wendy's grace and Wesley's meekness.

He wasted no time feeling around the room for the piano. As I carefully guided him to the bench, I sat right next to him. I gently put my hands on top of his and told him, "As I push down on your fingers, you play the keys." He caught right onto that, and in no time, he played his first simple song in a five-finger position. I removed my hands, and he played it over and over. That first lesson with Wesley went very well. He left that day, and I was amazed at how quickly he caught on. Wesley was born blind and had never seen the beautiful ocean he lived near or his beautiful mother Wendy.

The next week, Wendy let him come in on his own. I must admit I was a little nervous about this, but he found the piano, climbed on the bench, and played the song we had learned, plus some he had made up. He played the keys rather hard, so I had to help him gently push the keys down and curve his fingers. He would rock to the rhythm with his body.

This week, I decided to teach him a song he already knew from the church where he went with his parents. I sang the words gently to "Jesus Loves Me," and he told me he knew that song. In one lesson, he not only learned the right hand but the left hand with chords. I was so amazed at how quickly he caught on. I looked forward to his lesson every week. We became friends and laughed together about funny things and ate candy after the lessons. He was the sunshine of my week.

Wesley had never seen colored Christmas lights or a manger scene or even the beauty of a Christmas tree with all its ornaments of every color. He had heard the music and knew there was excitement in the air during this season, but he was not sure why. He loved the presents, though he could not see the beautiful wrapping paper or the shiny bows on the packages. He knew there was something to celebrate but was not fully understanding of it.

Wesley was not only sight-blind but was blind to the love of God through Jesus. As we began to learn "Silent Night," I had ask his mom if she thought he was a believer in Jesus yet. She said, "I do not know, but will you talk with him?"

I said, "I would love to."

I chose "Silent Night" as one of his performance songs. As we began to work on it, I told him the story of the Savior born at Christmas. I asked him if he knew why Jesus was born in the manger.

He said, "What's a manger?"

"Oh, well, it's a bed of hay they feed horses or cattle in."

"What do you mean by that?" he said so curiously. He had no idea about many of the things seeing people take for granted.

I had talked to many kids about Christmas and Jesus, but never one without sight. I felt lost. So then I prayed quietly to the Lord for help. How could I explain this beautiful scene of Christmas and the love of God to him?

So I just simply said, "Wesley, God loves you, and He sent Jesus from heaven to die for our sins on a cross!"

Then Wesley said, "What's a cross?"

"Oh me," I said to myself. So I went and got two pencils to form a cross and let him feel how to form a cross. Making a cross out of pencils was more confusing to him. And then I said, "They nailed Jesus to a cross."

Wesley asked, "What's a nail?" Frustrated by my own lack of knowing how to communicate this without visuals, I prayed and thought about what made me trust Christ as my Savior. It was hearing of God's love for me, a serious little sinner. I knew I must get him to understand God's love.

"Wesley," I said lovingly, "God loves you. He died to take away your sins."

Wesley began to cry. *Oh, me what have I done?* I thought. "Wesley what's wrong? What did I say?" But he continued to cry. I repeated, "God loves you." Then the crying became sobbing. "Wesley, it's okay. God loves you," I calmly said to him.

Wesley said, with tears and sobbing, "I hate them! God cannot love someone who hates kids and people. I could never go to heaven."

"What are you talking about, Wesley?" I said.

"I hear what they say and how they make fun of me. I am not deaf, just blind. And how they talk about my poor mom having a blind kid. I hear it all and I hate them! One kid took my cane at school and hid it. And the other kids laughed at me. God cannot love me because I am so bad and full of hate!" shouted Wesley through his tears.

I just held him and said, "God loves you even when you hate them! God loves you, Wesley, no matter what. I am bad too at times, and sometimes I sin and think evil of others in my heart, but God loves me and sent Jesus to die for my bad thoughts. He took my bad and gives me His love. Believe in His love, Wesley. God loves Wesley," I said with all the kindness and emotion I could.

He quit crying slowly, and I continued to hold his hands. I told him how sorry I was that people could be so cruel. I told him that I knew his pain was deep, but so was God's love for him.

When Wesley stopped crying, he said, "Why would Jesus do that for me?"

I said, "I do not know, but He did it for me and my sins too. He loves us, Wesley!" I began to quote: "For God so loved the world that He gave His one and only Son that whosoever believeth in Him should not perish but have everlasting life" (John 3:16).

And all of a sudden, he just said quietly, "I believe. I believe in Jesus and thank You, God, for loving me. Thank You for loving me. I am so sorry I hate them!"

That day, Wesley's eyes may have been blind, but he was not blind anymore to the love of God! I placed my hands on his eyes and told him that one day, the first face he would ever see would be Jesus, who loved him and gave His life for him. For all eternity, Wesley would be able to see Him and all the amazing things of heaven.

And with that, we finished learning to play "Silent Night." Wesley and I were teacher, student, and friends for several years. He became an amazing pianist and grew in the grace of his Lord and Savior Jesus Christ.

The Enemy with the Fence

As we pulled into the driveway to check out the house, I noticed something only this house had that none of the other houses did. I did not think much about it at that time, as I was excited about the fact that we might be able to buy our first house in a nice neighborhood. It was just what we needed and more, with a large backyard for our kids to play in.

Within a few weeks, we were moving in, and we were so happy to have a home to share with others. After we settled in, I thought it would now be a good time to start a Bible class for the kids in the neighborhood. We had a garage, and it would be perfect to use and decorate. Kids were everywhere on our street.

The neighbor on one side would always watch us out the window. It was a little scary, as we would see the curtain move as we went in and out. We tried to be friendly, but Mrs. War-dell did not want any friends. We were told that she was very mean to everyone. But we were up for this challenge. Hurt people seem to hurt other people, and maybe she just needed some unconditional love. I just did not know how much she was going to need.

As the day of excitement came for our first Bible Club, I was looking forward to the kids arriving. The garage was decorated with kids' things. The carpet pieces were on the floor to sit on, the candy bowl was full of all kinds of sweets, and the cookies and punch were ready to serve.

As the kids came from both directions, I never dreamed what would happen. The thing between Mrs. War-dell's house and ours was a fence. It went between our houses to the edge of the sidewalk.

There were a few children walking on the sidewalk when one stepped onto Mrs. War-dell's grass. I noticed her standing in the door but never dreamed what she would do. She threw open her door and starting yelling in an angry voice. "Get off my grass, get off my grass, and get off my grass!" The children were startled and scared, and so was I. I gently told them to stay on the sidewalk.

I did speak back at her and said, "We are sorry Mrs. War-dell." She then moved further into the yard and told me a few things I cannot repeat. My heart melted, and I continued to smile and encourage the kids to come into the garage.

The war was on with Mrs. War-dell, and that was her real name. When Bible Club was over, she stood on her porch just waiting for some kid to step on her grass. I guided their paths so as not to engage in her a war of the grass. But it had only just begun.

The next Friday came, and more kids were coming as the word got around. For every friend they invited, they got to go into the candy bowl and pick five extra pieces of candy. We doubled in one week, and I was so excited. This time, I was ready and waiting on the sidewalk and encouraging the kids not to step on her grass.

The curtains moved, and the door opened. She began to yell at me and say things I cannot repeat. I spoke up and told her not to talk to me or the children that way, adding that she did not own the sidewalk. She said she did and I had no right to have kids coming to my house. Now, that did it! My red hair went on fire, and I was so mad at her. I calmed myself down, knowing that this was a work of Satan to discourage these children from knowing the things of God.

She stayed on the porch till all the kids settled inside the garage. We started singing, and then the phone rang and rang and rang. I finally had to answer it, and guess who it was? Mrs. War-dell. She said we were too loud and to be quiet or she would call the police. My red hair was smoking now, and I just hung up. Would she really do that? I collected my thoughts again and continued to have club. Now I understood the fence. It was her way of keeping people away from her. I could see her anger, and now I had to learn how to love my enemy next door, not only through a fence but also through walls of anger and hurt.

This went on for weeks, and she did call the police, who drove by, waved at me, and smiled. I was a little scared, but after he smiled and waved, I figured he was on my side. The phone rang every week until I finally took it off the hook during club. We had fifty or more kids coming, and the other neighbors were thrilled the kids had something fun to look forward to. I was not the only neighbor whom she attacked with her mean spirit and words. God had a plan in putting me, who loved people, next door to a woman who could not stand people.

My husband and I did random acts of kindness toward Mrs. War-dell. We had seen her struggle to mow her lawn, and my husband would just go mow it. She would peek out between the curtains and watch. She never said thank you or anything as he did this many times. We found out she was on a fixed income, and we would send over groceries in my daughter's little red wagon. The girls would just set them on the porch, as she would not answer the door. She would take them in, as the next morning they were always gone.

One time, when my oldest daughter was pulling the wagon with a fresh, hot meal in it, she looked back at me and said, "Mommy, is she going to eat me?"

I said, "No, honey, she is not. I promise." Teaching my girls to love their enemy was something I had never dreamed would be so close to our home. God used this in so many ways in my own life and in the lives of the kids that came to Bible Club. I told the children we needed to love her, not hate her. After a few weeks, I had the children cross the street and not go near her yard to honor her. I would have to watch for traffic, as some kids were even dropped off by their parents.

Things seemed to settle down with her as we continued throughout the year to do acts of kindness. We would even pull the weeds in the fence between us. She was always watching, and then one day, I was taking over some hot sweet bread to leave on her porch when the door opened. I was a little startled! She said, "Do you want to come in?"

"Well, I guess I have to go get my girls."

"Okay," Mrs. War-dell said.

I went and got my little girls, and I said to the girls, "Do not touch anything, and sit quietly." As she was waiting with the door open, we went in. I must admit I was a little concerned about this. It was dark inside and a bit messy, but we found a place to sit down. She knitted and had blankets all over the place. She handed me one and said, "I made this one for you."

I was shocked and said, "Thank you so much!" She then asked if the girls could have a piece of candy, and I said, "Yes, they can." We talked for a little while, and then I excused us and went home. I could not wait to tell my husband because he was helping love our enemy.

No more did she yell or fuss about the kids. And I continued to have the kids cross over and honor her wishes. And we continued to take her food from time to time. She was lonely, afraid, and empty. And God put us next door to help her, and she helped us. She began to buy candy and hand it over the fence for the kids. She even smiled at me.

One day, she called to say she had finished a blanket for us and asked me to come over. On this visit, I asked Mrs. War-dell about her life story. She began to tell me about how hard life had been and how she had been so hurt along the way. I told her how sorry I was for her and began to understand more of the fence. The fence was her way of stopping people from hurting her anymore. It helped block out some of what might happen if people crossed over her way.

I waited till the next time we visited and told her about the love of Jesus. I told her that the Bible tells us the greatest love story. Jesus died on the cross for the sins of the whole world. I told her that we all had sinned against God. We read the Bible together, and she began to cry. After we went through John 3:16 together and I told her how much God loved her, she accepted Christ as her Savior that day. We were now on the same side. No longer enemies but sisters in Christ. From that day forward, things changed with us. Out of her little income, she saw to it that I had cookies and candy each week.

God loved Mrs. War-dell so much and wanted her to know that! God wanted me to love my enemy and do well to those who hate us.

Timmy the Terror

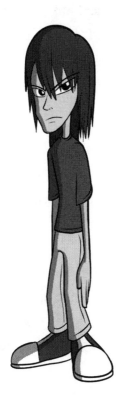

Upon moving to a new neighborhood, I needed to find some new piano students. So I decided to run an ad in the local newspaper. I also prayed that God would send me the students He wanted me to have.

The day the ad ran, I waited with anticipation for someone to call. The phone rang early, and a mom on the other end spoke about her oldest son and his talent, and how he needed a new teacher for piano. After we agreed to meet, she came over with Timmy.

Timmy was ten years old and seemed to be rather quiet. I could not see his eyes through the long hair draping over his face. He did not say much, but I could see his mother knew he had talent. She wanted this for Timmy, but I was not sure Timmy wanted this for himself. But we agreed to start his lessons the following week.

The afternoon came, and Timmy walked from his house, which was a short distance away. As he came in and sat down, I asked him to play me something from the books he had brought from his previous teacher. It was okay, but there was not much passion. As I gave him some instruction, he just glared at me. He did not like my instruction. I could see this was not going to be easy.

After each suggestion, he would look from under his long hair and resist. I quietly thought, *So this is why the other teacher dropped him as a student.*

After a few minutes of this, I just said, "Do you want to do this?"

He said belligerently, "Yes!"

"So what's the problem?" I said kindly.

"I do not know," he said.

"Well, play me something you like," I told him.

All of a sudden, he played a New Orleans blues song. I was

amazed, and because we lived in Louisiana, I was even more excited. I now realized this young kid had some amazing talent, but as a teacher who knew how much better he could be, I now faced his unteachable attitude.

His mother saw his rare talent, and she wanted to encourage that in Timmy. But as a young teacher myself, I did not know how to handle this. Timmy left that day with his head down. After pondering this, I decided I would give this one more try the next week. If he continued not to be teachable, then I would call his mother and let her know I was not the teacher for him.

The afternoon came. Timmy showed up on time, and we started again. I tried to be open with him and even offered him some candy before the lesson. I just tried to talk a little to him.

Timmy told me that he was the oldest of four brothers, and he took care of the other three after school until his parents got home from work. I could see how unhappy he was with life, but I also had realized in this short time that under that long hair, there was a kid searching for something.

We started his lesson, and immediately his bad attitude showed up again. I finally just said, "Timmy, this is not going to work! You do not want to let me guide you, so this will be our last time together. I will call your mom and let her know."

The previous week when I met his mom, I had given witness to the fact that I was a believer in Jesus and I shared this with my students. I had even given his mom a small book on what I believed. She was fine with that and spoke of where she went to church.

I could sense Timmy did not want me calling his mom. So, thinking I would not see him again, I decided to ask him a question about his church and his faith. I simply said, "Timmy, if you were to die, would you go to heaven?"

He looked right up at me from under his long hair and just said, "No!"

I said, "Would you like to know how to get to heaven?" I knew the church that his mom went to taught that you had to do laws to get to heaven. He had even gone to a school that taught this.

He started to talk to me. "I lay awake at night knowing if I die I am going to hell."

I said, "I am so sorry." So I just told him that he did not have to do that and I could show him some verses from the Bible on how he could know he could go to heaven.

He said sternly, "Show me!"

I opened my Bible, which was nearby on a table, and read to him the verse that says, "Verily, verily I say unto you, he that believeth on me [Jesus] hath everlasting life" (John 6:47). Timmy took the Bible and read it for himself. He had heard the story of Christ and how He had died for sins, was buried, and rose, but he had not seen the simple truth that he needed to receive this gift of salvation from Him.

"What about good works to get me to heaven? I have to be good. And I cannot do that."

So I turned to Ephesians 2:8–10 and read it to him. "For by grace are you saved through faith and that not of yourselves it is the gift of God not of works lest any man should boast. For we are His workmanship created in Christ Jesus unto good works which God has before ordained that we should walk in them." And once again, Timmy wanted to read it for himself.

We started to talk now, and he became open with me. His bitter attitude was gone. He was searching for some peace. I told him how God loved him and died to pay for his sins. He knew that, but he did not know how to have a relationship with this loving God who had sent His Son Jesus to die for his sins. I told him that he needed to receive Christ as his forever Savior and that would begin his relationship with this loving God. That day, sitting on the piano bench, he did. I prayed with him and told him to read the same book I had given his mom.

I did tell him I was going to call his mom and let her know that we had talked. He asked intently, "Are you going to stop teaching me?"

I said, "No, but I am going to pray about it, and we will see. I want to teach you, but you have to let me do that, teach you!" Timmy nodded his head. There was a change in him, and as he left that day, I invited him to the Kids' Bible Club on Friday at my house.

Timmy showed up on Friday, and I noticed that some of the kids who had been coming for a while stared at him and stayed away. *What was that all about?* I thought.

That week, I asked one of my neighbor kids who came over often about Timmy. She said, "He is known as Timmy the Terror."

I said, "What do you mean?"

She said, "He fights with everyone because they pick on him

and his brothers. We are all scared of him, and he has that long hair and he looks weird." So now I had a little more information about Timmy and his life.

That week, when he came to his piano lesson, he was different. The first thing he said was, "I read that little book you gave to my mom."

"Great what did you think?" I asked him.

"It made sense to me." Timmy was a very logical thinker, and he understood the message in it. The message was about how God loved him and sent Jesus to be his Savior. He had believed now that Jesus died for his sins. It was no longer simply a fact to him, but now his faith. He now had begun a relationship with the God who loved him. There was a new peace about him!

As we began his piano lesson, I realized that this teacher was going to have to rethink her teaching ability. So I talked to him about how we were going to do this. "What songs do you want to learn?" I asked him. He named a few. I told him we would make a deal. "If you do fifteen minutes of what I want, then we will do fifteen minutes of what you want." He liked that idea. And off we went.

With a new peace about him, he became a great piano student and musician, but there is more to Timmy's story.

Timmy Takes a Turn

In our previous story of Timmy the Terror, we heard of how Timmy had now begun a relationship with his Father God through receiving Christ as his Savior. His faith was real to him, and he had a new purpose. The problem was that the reputation he had for being a terror and fighting was still there. He had much to learn, as you will see in this story.

Timmy had three brothers younger than him, and he was very protective of them. But sometimes, his way of protecting and defending them got him into trouble.

Because I lived in the neighborhood that was close to the elementary school, there were always a lot of kids around. One day, around the time that school let out, I heard some noise down the street. The kids were running and saying, "Fight, fight, fight!" This was before I met Timmy, and all I knew was that it was a kid fighting about something someone said about one of his brothers. As I walked toward the corner, everyone started running.

When I asked what the fight was about, one of the kids said, "It's Timmy the Terror, and someone called his little brother Four-Eyes!"

I said, "Well, that is sad!"

"He gave the boy a black eye who called his brother that!" called out another kid.

One day, it came to my mind that that fighter was "Timmy the Terror," who now was my friend and student. I asked him one day about that, and he said, "Yes, it was me."

So I said, "Do you still do that?"

"Well I try not to now, but kids expect me to fight for my brothers."

I spoke up and firmly said, "No, not anymore. The Lord does not want you to do that anymore. You need to walk away. I mean it, Timmy. You are different now. No more fighting."

He looked at me at said, "Okay, Mrs. Sandra, I won't." And he did not fight anymore. The kids at Bible Club noticed a difference in time.

It was not easy for Timmy, but he knew that it was not right anymore. Then he got picked on for going to Bible Club and being different. God had got a hold on him, and he was trying to do right. I told him often how proud I was of him.

Timmy brought his three little brothers to Kids' Bible Clubhouse. There were Wayne, David, and little Bruce. Bruce was the one with the glasses whom Timmy had gotten into the fight over. He bought them every week and made them sit up and listen. In time, each one of them also received Christ as his Savior. The youngest one, Bruce, was so special to me. Bruce always sat close to Timmy. I was impressed with Timmy and how he cared for his younger brothers. When they would get candy every week, he made sure they said thanks.

One fall day, right after Timmy trusted Christ, there was a knock on my door. It was Timmy with a friend of his. Timmy had him by the shirt collar. The kid looked a little scared. I welcomed them in, and Timmy just said this, and I quote: "Tell him what you told me!"

I looked a little startled and with a smile said, "Well, let's have some candy first." So I ask his friend his name, and we talked a little bit. He and Timmy had been friends for a long time, and Timmy just wanted him to know what he had come to know about Christ. I had to tell Timmy that dragging his friend there by the shirt collar was not the way to share about Christ's love.

I shared with his friend about how God loved him, but I was not sure I got through. I did sow the seeds of the Word of God, and that does not return empty. He left, and I never saw him again. He probably ran when he got away from Timmy that day. I did tell Timmy, "That was great, bringing your friend, but next time, let him know a little bit more about why he is coming to see me." I told Timmy that he looked scared. He told me he had actually forced his friend to come, but had told him I would give him some candy. I asked him, "Did you tell him you were going to beat him up if he did not come?" I had to laugh at that, but Timmy was bold about his newfound faith and peace. This happened many times with Timmy, but from then on, he did not drag them to my door. Instead, he asked them to come get some candy from Mrs. Sandra. I thought, *Well, that's okay.*

He invited more kids to Kids' Bible Clubhouse than anyone. I think they were afraid he would beat them up if they did not come. Over time, Timmy changed, and kids actually liked him. He had a great sense of humor and became one of my helpers and encouragements weekly.

After I had known and taught Timmy for two years, he came in sadly one day to tell me he was moving. I had poured my life into him, and he was part of our family now. My girls loved him, and he and his brothers ate meals with us often. His piano skills had flourished. He told me he was moving to a place about thirty miles from there in the country.

His mom loved horses and Sheltie dogs, and they were going to move where they could have horses and more dogs.

I remember being so sad, not knowing what God had already planned for my family in the future with these four boys.

We said goodbye one day, and I actually cried as I hugged each of them. Little Bruce with the glasses also cried. My girls were sad also, as they felt like they were losing their big brother that played with them.

And then the day came one year later that the Lord found us a new place to live. A friend who was a realtor offered us a new home he would build for us. Guess where the new house was? Yes, you guessed it—God was moving us to them in the country. At first, I did not realize that this was where Timmy and his brothers had moved. But God who goes before and knows best brought us back together.

Sad Chad and Chatty Cathy

"Get up, Chad! It's time for school. I made your favorite chocolate chip pancakes. Hurry up so we can eat together before we both have to leave. I can't be late for work, and you do not want to miss the bus. I have warmed the maple syrup," called his mom.

Pulling the covers over his face, Chad said to himself, *Where I am today? It gets so confusing.* Ever since his parents had divorced, Chad would get confused sometimes as to whose house he was at. *Not fair,* he thought, *that a kid has to keep up with their crazy schedules. Well, I better hurry up, as those pancakes do smell good! Mom always does special things for me when I am at her house.* Chad called back to his mom, "Now I'm up!" As Chad got ready, he talked out loud to himself: "Where is my book bag?" and "This thing weighs a ton" and "Oh, no, I did not finish my homework" and "I know Mom is always too busy to help me." As he looked up to heaven, he said, "If there is a God, please help me!" And with that, he went downstairs for breakfast.

"Chad, why so sad?" said his mom.

He thought to himself, *Seriously, you don't get it. Yes, the pancakes are great, but I miss Dad so badly! Why did this happen to me?*

Mom said to Chad, "Tonight you go to your dad's."

"Okay." He nodded with another sad face. He thought within himself, *Yep, Dad's it is, and he is going to not want me to be sad either. I think my new name is just Sad Chad.*

As Chad waited for the school bus, he was hoping to just sit and stare out the window and be sad, but he knew that *she* would be on the bus, and she was so annoying. *If I just ignore her, she will go away,* he thought.

Oh no, here she comes! Help me! he groaned within himself.

"Hi, Chad! Can I sit here?"

I will just ignore her, said Chad to himself as Chatty Cathy sat down. "Well, I guess it's okay." She was always so happy, and she even smelled nice.

Every day, Chatty Cathy would try to cheer up Sad Chad. It was like a job to her to find out why Chad was sad, and day in and day out, he would not tell her. He was embarrassed about his parents. "Leave me alone," he would say under his breath, but that was not going to happen with Cathy.

Cathy had been given the gift of talking and smiling. One time, Cathy was told by her parents not to say anything as they were shopping for a car. "Just be quiet, please, Cathryn"—her parents called her Cathryn when they were serious.

She just could not. She looked up at the salesman and said with a smile, "I can tie my shoes!" Her parents just shook their heads.

The school bus arrived at school, and off everybody went to their classes. The unfortunate thing for Chad was that Chatty Cathy was in his class. All day, when he would look her way, she tried to make him smile. He was so annoyed. But he thought, *Why is she so happy? I wish I could be happy about something.*

Day after day, he endured her happiness until one day, he finally looked at her and said very sternly, "Why do you care if I am sad, Cathy? My parents do not care that I am sad, and I am sad and want to be left alone!"

With a smile on her face and kindness, she said, "Well, you are not alone, Chad. God is with you, and He loves you!" Chad was stunned by what she said, and with her smile, she went on her way, leaving Chad to think about what she said.

He thought about that all day long, and as he stared at her in class, she kindly smiled at him. He even did not mind her sitting next to him on the bus that afternoon. He did not say much to Chatty Cathy, but it seemed what she had said made him feel somewhat better.

He kept thinking, *God loves me, and I am not alone. I feel so alone at times, but she says God loves me. Maybe He does care. I did ask God to help me.* Maybe "Chatty Cathy," as he called her, had more to say about God.

The strangest thing was the next day, when he got on the bus, he was hoping she would sit next to him. He had a little hope that day would be better. He even looked at her with a half smile. She, with her happy heart, had made him feel better. Chad thought to himself, *I am going to talk to her now, but what do I say?*

That day and what she said meant so much to him. So Chad asked her on the way home that day, "Cathy, what do you mean, God is with me?"

"Well," Cathy said, "God loves you and wants to be your friend. He knows why you are sad, even though you will not tell me. It bothers me because I have been very sad too, and God helped me through giving me Jesus as my friend. I have learned to be glad even when I am sad, Chad. And you can know Jesus as your friend too."

Then it was time to get off the bus, and he turned to Chatty Cathy for the first time and said, "See you tomorrow!" And he got off the bus.

He was at his dad's that night, and as he lay in bed, he kept thinking about what she had said, over and over. *God loves me and cares, and I have heard a little about Jesus, as I went to church with my friend one time. I need to know more about Jesus and God. Jesus wants to be my friend. I do not have many friends. Oh well, I cannot wait to talk to Cathy some more.* And with that, Chad went off to sleep.

When morning came, Chad was ready to get up and go to school. He had a little hope and was looking forward to sitting with Cathy on the bus, but she was not there that day. He was truly sad. He was missing his annoying friend, and for several days, Cathy was not there. When he asked at school, nobody knew where she was.

And then Cathy was back, and Chad was glad. He even asked her to sit with him on the bus. "Where were you?"

"Oh, well, I got really sick, so I have just been home, and I am still not feeling well yet," said Cathy quietly.

"Wow, I thought you had died or something!"

"Oh, do not worry about that, Chad! If I die, I am going to heaven, because Jesus is my Savior!"

"What did you say, Cathy? You know you are going to heaven? Nobody knows that," said Chad.

"Well, I do, and many other people do too," said Cathy.

The bus arrived at school, and off they went for the day. Chad was more curious than ever now and just kept wondering how she could say that she knew she was going to heaven. That afternoon, she did not ride the bus home, as her mom picked her up to go back to the doctor. Chad was really missing his chatty friend now. She was not so annoying anymore.

So that night, he lay in bed and thought about the things she had said. *God loves me? Jesus cares and wants to be my friend? Cathy knows she is going to heaven!*

The weekend was coming, and he could not even remember

where he was going with his dad or mom. He just wanted to talk more with Cathy. On the bus the next day, he asked her, "What are you doing this weekend, Cathy?"

"Well, I am going to my church. Do you want to come?" she asked.

Startled by her request, he said, "I guess I will have to ask my dad. I think I am with him this weekend."

Okay, here is my mom's cell phone number," she replied as she wrote it down for him. "Just call, and we can pick you up." With that, happy Cathy hopped off the bus for class.

As soon as he got to his dad's, he asked if he could go with Cathy to church. His dad said," Yes, if she picks you up, that is fine. I used to go to church when I was a kid."

He asked his dad, "Why don't we go now, Dad?"

"Well, Sundays it's busy with football and other stuff to do." With that, Chad made the call, and the plan was set to go with Cathy to church.

Sunday came, and Chad was anxious while waiting. He did not know what to expect, but he knew with Cathy he would not have to talk much, so he was good with that. He was kind of shy. Cathy's mom, dad, and brother came in to meet his dad. They seemed really nice. They asked if Chad could go to lunch with them afterward, and his dad said "Yes, I will be here watching the game." And with that, they left.

Upon arriving, Chad and Cathy went off to a thing called children's church, where all the kids were. The room was filled with boys and girls, the walls were painted with bright colors, and some fun music was playing. Then, of course, Cathy was introducing him to all her friends. She had a lot of friends.

After the fun music stopped, a lady got up with a book in her hands. She called it the Bible, and Chad actually had seen one of those at his grandparents' house. He had wondered what it was about. She opened it and read a story from it, John 3:1–18. Then she told the story so the class could understand it better.

She said, "This story is about a man who quietly walked through the streets of Jerusalem one night looking for Jesus. He found Him and did not want the rulers he served with to know that he was going to talk to Jesus. He was a Pharisee and a very important religious leader. Nicodemus was his name, and he told Jesus that the miracles He did showed that He was a teacher sent from God. No man could do those miracles unless God was with him."

"Jesus told the man that he needed to be born again. Nicodemus asked, "How can a man be born again when he is old?" The kind teacher explained that when you are born the first time, you become a human, and with that comes a sinful nature that separates us from God. Sin is when we choose to disobey God's commands like "Do not lie, steal, or disobey your parents." Chad knew he had done those things, and this was a very interesting story.

As he listened, she continued to tell how God is not pleased with our sin, but He loves us so much that He was willing to send His one and only Son Jesus to die in our place, so one day when we die we can go to heaven, where there is no sin. Jesus told Nicodemus that he must be born again by receiving a new birth, and that only comes when he believes in Jesus as his Savior.

Nicodemus listened intently to Jesus, and He even used the wind as an illustration. Jesus said, "You cannot see the wind, but you know it's there. So it is with those who are born of the spirit, those who trust Christ as their Savior. The Holy Spirit comes within to live." Jesus wanted Nicodemus to know that doing good works would not get him to heaven, as the Pharisees taught people. Jesus continued to tell him, "God so loved the world that He gave his only Son, that whosoever believeth in Him should not perish but have everlasting life" (John 3:16).

The teacher continued, "When we ask Jesus to forgive all our sins, Jesus is able to save us from going to hell and will take us to heaven when we die. In heaven, there is no sin, not a lie or anything bad like pain or sadness. Heaven is the most beautiful place, where the street is paved with gold and gates are made of pearl and precious jewels of every color line the walls." Chad thought, *I truly want to go there if there is no sadness.* Sad Chad was beginning to see why Chatty Cathy was so happy. She had heaven to look forward to, Jesus was her friend, and God did love her and him.

The teacher closed with the words that Jesus told Nicodemus that night. John 3:16 says, "For God so loved the world (that's everybody) that He gave His one and only Son (Jesus), that whosoever believes in Him should not perish (go to hell) but have everlasting life (heaven)."

In a quiet, serious voice, she asked them to close their eyes and pray. "Have you ever put your faith in Jesus Christ to be your Savior? Ask Jesus to forgive you of your sins. You can do that right now! God loves you so much that He sent His Son, Jesus Christ, to make the payment needed to take away your sin so you can be born again. Born into the forever family of God. Jesus took your punishment for all your sins—past, present, and future. Jesus not only died but also was buried in a tomb and rose again. He says you will also rise from the dead when you die if you trust Him right now. Will you do that? Eternal life is His gift to you."

Sad Chad prayed to God and did receive the gift of eternal life in heaven that day. His deep sadness went away. He had a peace that came from knowing God loved him, and Jesus was his new friend. With eyes open, he looked at Chatty Cathy and was happy she was his friend who did not give up on him when he was not always kind to her.

Chad continued to come with Cathy to church, where he learned more about how Jesus cared about him and his sadness. He began to pray for his parents and that they too would come to know his friend Jesus. He was still sad Chad at times, but Jesus, his new friend, was always with him, and Jesus brought some true happiness to his life.

What a friend he found in Jesus, who was always there to listen and just hang out with him when he was feeling sad. He still hurt about his parents, but he learned how to love them despite his pain. He knew we are all sinners and have a hard time loving each other sometimes.

Even parents cannot always be there to help you, but Jesus always will be. Everyone needs a Chatty Cathy in his or her life that talks too much. At least she talks about the things that matter. That is Jesus.

The C Word

C is a letter in the alphabet that a lot of good words start with. C for candy, so sweet and wonderful to the taste. C is also for chocolate which melts in your mouth. C is for cars that boys love to play with and dream one day of driving. C is for cats that are loveable and for cake with white icing that is so thick you just want to lick it all. C is for Christmas, the best time of the year, celebrating the birth of our Savior, Jesus.

There is another *C* word that is not so good. I know this word well and wish I did not. When we hear it, our hearts are filled with fear and the unknown. The sad look on someone's face when the doctor says you have this *C* word.

This *C* word is cancer. Have you heard it? Even as I write this, I know of children, dads, moms, grandparents, husbands, wives, and all people today that could get the *C* word, and it is the most tragic *C* word I know. It has come into my life several times in the last few years. It has brought many tears to my eyes and many prayers lifted up to God.

Do you know of someone who has this? Or, sadly, maybe you? It takes great courage to fight this word, and I have seen firsthand how hard those who have this *C* word fight against this fear-filled word taking control of their bodies. *Cancer* is defined as a serious and at times deadly disease. Abnormal cells take on a growth of their own and sometimes cannot be stopped. Cancer is like sin that is not controlled. Once a person trusts Christ as his or her Savior, the Holy Spirit gives that person power to control sin in his or her life. Sometimes, drugs and the power of prayer will take this *C* word and destroy what damage it has done or will do.

It brings tears and pain for those fighting. I have filled many a bottle with tears over this *C* word. Those who are standing alongside people battling this must provide great care, love, and hope to help all defeat it. So much is being done all over the world to research and help fight this *C* word. People pray. God hears and heals many from this sickness here on earth, and they live to do great things.

I sat by my best friend, who had this disease. As I watched him fight so hard to stay here in this world, he fought a good fight of faith. He was a faithful servant of his Lord Jesus. His pain and suffering were so great, but he and I found joy along the way. Not wasting any time here, he shared with others what would be ahead for him when he died. He was going home to meet his forever friend Jesus, who gave His life for him.

My best friend knew that in Revelation 21:4 of the Bible, it said that God would wipe away the sad things, and there would be no more death, sorrow, pain, or tears. We shed many tears together. My best friend could not defeat the C word of cancer, and he left and went to heaven in my presence. He is healed forever in the arms of Jesus, his Savior. I miss him, but I am hoping he is having some C word angel food *cake* up there. I will join him one day to eat cake together.

Then there is the C word that gives eternal hope and forever healing. *Christ,* the Lord Jesus, did not die from cancer, but He died for those who have it. He too suffered great pain as He was hung there on a C word "cross". He died to take away the sins of the whole world. He offers an eternal home called heaven, where there is no pain. This is a gift from God for anyone who believes in the name of Jesus Christ. His name means "God my Savior, my keeper and my defender." "For the payment of sin is death, but the gift of God is eternal life through Jesus Christ our Lord" (Romans 6:23).

No one gets cancer because he or she sinned or did anything wrong. We live in a world where sickness and death happen. For those who receive Jesus Christ as their personal Savior, their final home is heaven, where no C word *cancer* exists. He came to take away the pain forever in a place called heaven. Christ died, was buried, and rose, proving He had power over death. After Jesus died, before He left us here, He gave us these comforting words: "In my Father's house are many mansions, if it were not so I would have told you. I go to prepare a place for you" (John 14:2). And in His love letter to us, the Bible, we find this C word, *comfort*: "And God shall wipe away all tears from their eyes; and there shall be no more death, neither sorrow, nor crying, neither shall there be any more pain: for the former things are passed away" (Revelation 21:4). Heaven is real and prepared for those who believe in Jesus as their Savior. Do you believe? I hope so!

I was walking behind my daughter and son-in-law on a rainy day in New York City just a few years ago. Their blue umbrella covered them. Arm in arm they walked, not knowing if they together would see their three young children grow up. We stopped at a quaint restaurant to eat a wonderful breakfast on our way to the hospital and actually had some laughter. The C word cancer had invaded my son-in-law's body, but it could not kill their joy or peace in the midst of great uncertain times. They both knew God loved them and had accepted Jesus as their Lord and Savior.

Their three small children were home, praying that Daddy would be healed. I remember one night so vividly: as the children saw their dad suffering, their precious faces were filled with fear and sadness. And they prayed diligently for their daddy to be healed.

My thoughts were: would my son-in-law be there to walk my granddaughter down the aisle one day when she got married? Would he get to see his two little boys become the men of God he dreamed they would be one day?

God has healed my son-in-law of his cancer now for many years. His children are growing up quickly and every day with Jesus. Being cancer-free is a gift to his family and to me. He is a special person, and my caregiver daughter rejoices every new day they are given. They eat a lot of the other *C* words to celebrate, like cake and hot chocolate for every Christmas they celebrate, another year cancer free.

As I ponder these things, I am so thankful for the hope of eternal life. As I have seen with my own eyes, when loved ones with this *C* word leave this world, I know I will see them again because they had put their faith in the *C* word Christ.

"These things have I written unto you that believe on the name of the Son of God that you may know that you have eternal life, and that **you** may believe on the name of the Son of God" (1 John 5:13).

For God is a healer here on earth, and He hears the prayers of His children who ask for healing. So many people have been healed of the *C* word cancer. Doctors all over the world know the healing of God. They cannot explain many times when the hand of God reaches into a body and heals it. We know that doctors are given wisdom and medicine to help heal, and this all comes from God.

As Solomon, king of Israel, wrote to his son, "My son, pay attention to what I say; listen closely to my words. Do not let them out of your sight keep them within your heart; for they are life to those who find them and health to a man's whole body" (Proverbs 4:20–22).

And also remember the words of David: "Then they cried to the LORD in their trouble, and He saved them from their distress. He sent forth His word and healed them; He rescued them from the grave. Let them give thanks to the LORD for His unfailing love and His wonderful deeds for men" (Psalm 107:19–20).

So, since I am still here celebrating the life I have, I think I will go and have some of the good and delicious C words like chocolate, cake, and oh yes, my favorite caramel. "Oh taste and see that the Lord is good, blessed in the one who puts their trust in Him!" (Psalms 34:8).

Gifted

"F sharp," said Clara to the man in the music store. She was standing behind the beautiful, black, shiny piano, and what she said took the man by surprise. He looked down at her and smiled. Clara was only four years old. The man continued the game she had started by playing other notes. Each one Clara called out correctly without seeing the keys. This was truly a gift of music that Clara did not understand; she just thought this was fun.

The salesman looked at Clara and kindly said, "One day, you are going to be a great pianist!" The girl's mother realized right then that there was something very special about her little girl. They left the store, and all day, Clara's mom kept thinking about what he had said. Could it be Clara was given the gift of perfect pitch? *Truly, God, who designed her, would give this special child to me,* her mom thought.

That evening, Mom shared with Clara's father what had happened that day. Father agreed with Mom's thoughts about Clara's ability and future with music. In Clara's home, there was a piano, but it was very old and not the best for someone who had perfect pitch to practice on. That was why Mom was looking at new pianos that day in the music store. Mom played piano but wanted something better for her daughter. She remembered one day when, as she was playing and struggling to read music, she had looked up to heaven and said, "Lord, if you give me children, please give them the gift of music." And it seemed He had done that.

It was not long before Clara had a new, shiny piano. Her piano lessons started, and it all seemed so easy, except for reading the music. She would say, "Play it, Mom," since her mom was her first piano teacher. Once Clara heard a piece, she could play it right back. She was given a special gifting by God, who designed her, but she would need years of piano lessons and lots of practice to make this gift the best for the glory of God.

Clara worked hard, with hours and hours of practice. When she was a teenager, Mom bought her a piano for her room. Her love of music grew deeper the more she fell in love with her God and Savior Jesus Christ. She loved performing, but her passion for God drove her to use it all for the glory of God. She became a songwriter, and churches have used her music to worship her master and king, Jesus. Clara even learned to play guitar, and once again, her passion was stirred. She always used her gift to lift up the name of Jesus, her Savior.

Then there was beautiful Annie. Annie was born a savant. Although she was blind and could only hear a little out of one ear, she had the extraordinary gift hearing sounds of music and duplicating them without error. People looked at Annie as if she were not all there, but in reality, she was designed by God to be more than we can explain. There were only a few savants in the world, and Annie was one of them. In her earliest years, Annie could play Bach, Beethoven, and any other song she could hear. She could even compose her own original songs at five years old.

Annie was looked upon as disabled, but that was not true in God's view of things. She had ability beyond what scientists and doctors could explain. Her mom knew when she was born that she was special to God. Annie lives for her God, and when she plays, all glory goes to Him.

We are all uniquely and wonderfully made. God makes no mistakes, for He is over all and in all. You must find what is unique about you. Do you know what that is? Ask God for His gifts. King Solomon asked for a gift, and God granted that gift to him: wisdom and knowledge. Second Chronicles 1:10 says, "Give me now wisdom and knowledge, that I may go out and come in before this people; for who can judge this, thy people, who are so great?"

"For you created my inmost being; you knit me together in my mother's womb. I praise you because I am fearfully and wonderfully made; your works are wonderful, I know that full well. My frame was not hidden from you when I was made in the secret place" (Psalm 139:13–15a).

Any abilities or so-called disabilities are given to us for one reason. They are given to bring glory to God. We are the light of the world, and whatever we are given, it is to shine for His glory. God makes no mistakes in the mother's womb. When He met a man who was born blind, Jesus reminded His disciples that even what appeared to be this man's disability was intended for the glory of God.

Samson in the Bible was given superhuman strength. He had remarkable strength, and Samson today would have been called a superhuman. There are many such athletes today who are given some of what Samson had. Many give glory to God for their ability and tap into God's strength for more. Samson was strong as long as he kept obeying God, but when he quit doing that, his strength was taken away.

Athletes are admired for their determination, perseverance, and skills. Many have other disabilities but overcome them with the ability to push past the things that hinder them and march into victory.

Nathan was told as a child that he would not be able to walk or run due to a rare disease that he had. But in his heart, he knew that God had a purpose for him, and it was to be a soccer player. He watched games on TV every time he could. He tried hard to kick around a soccer ball and determined in his heart that one day he would play soccer on a real field instead of just messing around inside his home.

There came the time in Nathan's life when he accepted God's Son Jesus to be his Savior. His parents took him to verses in the Bible where he read that Jesus had suffered on the cross for his sins. He had no problem admitting he had sin, for there were times when anger filled his heart. Nathan knew that this was wrong and that it was sin. He believed in Jesus and became a child of God. God now being his Heavenly Father was where he went to find strength to get better. He talked with God all the time. He had peace, which no one understood. He tapped into God's strength through accepting His Son Jesus. He loved this verse and would quote it this way: "For who is God except the Lord? Who but our God is a solid rock? God is my strong fortress, and He makes my way perfect" (2 Samuel 22:33).

Nothing could discourage Nathan's passion. He got up every day striving to walk, run, and get stronger. He also prayed for God's help and healing. God showed up and Nathan grew stronger, as his disability seemed to be not holding him back. Even his doctor was amazed at what was happening. For Nathan, it was no miracle—just determination and knowing God had a plan above what seemed to others as a disability became his ability to rise above all others' expectations.

Nathan did play soccer and went on to be one of the best on the field. He played to bring glory to God for helping him defeat what others said he could never overcome. His greatest ability was to defeat his disability, and that Nathan did.

And then there is Hannah. I met this beautiful, spectacular young girl a few years ago. Hannah was born with cerebral palsy and was in her wheelchair the day I met her. She had a contagious smile and arms that reached out to love you the best she could. Her eyes were the center of her heart, and when you looked into them, you could sense the longing she had to speak and tell you so many things.

Locked into her silent world, she longed to tell you what she was thinking. Hannah, when she was around worship of God, would always lift her hands the best she could in praise. No one doubted what she was doing, and she did not hold back like some of us do. Sometimes, I think her gift to me is watching her smile and worship. She makes some noise, but to God, it is a sweet sound to His ears. What a gift she has to brighten my day when I have the special privilege to see her. I must say that her parents have taught her the beauty of the gospel and that God makes no mistakes. Her disability is just for a short time here on Earth.

Hannah now has a computer and can communicate her words and thoughts. She received Jesus Christ as her Savior and was also baptized in the beautiful ocean off the island where she lives with her family. Her faith is strong, and her worship is real. Her gift of love and inspiring others to love her Jesus touches so many.

Hannah knows one day she will walk and talk with her Jesus. The first street Hannah will walk will be gold, and the first words she will speak will probably be "Jesus, my Jesus!"

So, *gifted* is a word full of options! We are all some kind of gift wrapped up to be opened by the love of God through Christ Jesus. Ask God to gift you in a way that will bring Him honor and glory to His name.

Weakness becomes strength when God becomes the focus. Strength becomes a weakness when God is not the focus. So, whether you are gifted with ability or your gift is a disability, it all can be used to glorify God.

"My grace is sufficient for you, my power is made perfect in weakness. Therefore I will boast all the more gladly about my weaknesses, so that Christ's power may rest on me. That is why, for Christ's sake, I delight in weaknesses, in insults, in hardships, in persecutions, in difficulties. For when I am weak, then I am strong" (2 Corinthians 2:9–10).

The Everlasting Guinea Pig

Day in and day out, this little guinea pig sat in his cage in the pet store. Children would come and stare at him, and he would sit looking up, hoping someone would take him home.

This little guinea pig had a problem, and you could not tell by looking at him. He looked like any other guinea pig, all cute and fuzzy. He was happy there in the cage in the pet store. He got good fresh food and water, and someone cleaned up his messy cage every day. Oh, the good life of this guinea pig.

One day, a happy family of four came in, and they went right to where this guinea pig's cage was. The little boy named Max was very interested in him. The boy smiled and chatted with his parents about him.

Max had wanted a guinea pig for a while. His parents had told him that after he finished school that year and did well, he could have one. This was a great time for Max to get him. His parents thought Max would have the summer to play with him and learn how to take care of him. Even his older sister was excited also about this new pet coming to live with them.

The decision was made. They went and got the pet store assistant and told him they were ready to buy the guinea pig and take it home. Max had to get a cage and all the things to make his new pet comfortable in its new home. Max held him and immediately fell in love with this little furry guy.

Max sat in the back seat with the little box with holes in it on his lap, peeking at him all the way home. Soon they got home, and he let him out in his room to play with him. He sort of just sat there. "Unusual," they thought. Max carried him around the house all the time.

Now they needed a name. So Max named him Chunk. A funny name, but he was a little chunk of a guinea pig already. Max set up the cage in his room and was so happy with his new friend. But Chunk was a little different, Max found out.

Chunk loved his fresh strawberries every morning and would squawk until Max fed him. Max would let him out to play with him, but oddly, he just sat there. He did not run around or play. He put him inside the wheel to play, and Chunk just sat there. This was strange, as normally guinea pigs like to run around the room and even hide. Not Chunk; he just sat there.

All summer when Max would get Chunk out to play with him, he would just sit, content to do nothing. He needed exercise, as he was getting really chunky. He got his food and his cage cleaned and was content to just sit, unlike most guineas.

Max would get him out and continue, year after year, to try to get him to do something, but Chunk just sat contently. He would make noise for his fresh strawberries. Year after year went by, and Max kept him in his room in his big cage now, which had rollers on it so he could move Chunk from room to room. After a while, Max was annoyed with Chunk and Chunk's personality disorder where he just sat day in and day out. It seemed he was going to live forever doing nothing. It was just not what Max had dreamed of when he wanted a pet to play with.

Years passed, and something very scary happened. Max and his family did not know how much they loved Chunk until an emergency happened.

Max's family lived near the ocean on an island. They heard that a big hurricane was headed right for their home on the island. The family had to evacuate in a hurry. They had to leave Chunk and his large cage behind. Max and his dad made sure they had filled up his water bottle and food to the top before they had to quickly get off the island. Max was sad but prayed, "God, take care of my friend Chunk until we get back home."

As Max stared out of the van window as they were pulling out of the driveway, he quietly said, "Goodbye, Chunk." The family had no idea when they would return, as this was a big hurricane. How long could Chunk go on the food and water he had?

Max and his family left the island across a long, tall bridge. It was a scary time for the family and so many others. Max wondered if others on the island had had to leave their pets also. They had their dog with them, but just could not take Chunk. His dad assured him Chunk would be okay.

The family went far off the island for safety, and the storm did hit the island. There was so much damage that people were not allowed back on the island for a week. Max was worried about Chunk. Even his dad was worried and wished they could have brought him with them.

Max trusted God that Chunk would be okay. After a week, Max's dad decided he would head back to the island where they lived. The family had no idea if their house had been damaged. He told Max, "As soon as I get there and find out about Chunk, I will call you."

His dad was able to get back on the island, and he began to see so much damage done by the hurricane. He could not wait to get to their home and see whether Chunk had survived the storm or run out of food and water and died. His anxious heart was getting the best of him. He cared deeply for his son and even his son's pet.

As he finally got through the debris in the roads and approached their home, it looked like it had been spared from serious damage. Lots of trees were down, and debris was everywhere, but his dad's big concern was Chunk. What would he find? And how was Max going to take it if Chunk the guinea pig had not survived the storm?

And then the time came as Max's dad opened the door and went first to check on Chunk. *Oh, no,* he thought as he looked into the cage. The house smelled horrible from something. And there was Chunk, not moving. The dad got tears in his eyes as he thought, *Chunk is dead, and he's not moving. How am I ever going to tell Max?*

But then his dad bumped the cage, and Chunk moved a little bit and opened his eyes. He was alive! He was alive and doing what he always did—*nothing!* Just sitting there being Chunk. His food was gone, but he still had water.

His dad called Max immediately and said, "Chunk is alive and doing what he always does, nothing but being the everlasting guinea pig with a personality disorder. Or just being Chunk, the way God made him."

We can learn from Chunk that being quiet and still is okay, knowing you are loved unconditionally just the way you are.

Cowboy Cole

Cole was a little boy with big dreams. He was born in the big state of Texas, and his parents owned a ranch. Horses and cattle were a way of life for him. His first memories were of watching his mom and dad load up his sister's horse and head out to rodeos on the weekends. His sister, Mallory, was one of the best barrel racers on the rodeo circuit. She was brave and would burst out with speed on her horse and circle those barrels quicker than anyone. Her runs were so fast, and Cole would sit in amazement on the bleachers and watch her go. He loved the dirt at the rodeo and would spend hours playing in it with his tractor each weekend.

As he got older, he began to ride the horses around his ranch. Cole's big dream as a little kid was to someday ride in the rodeo. His first pair of shoes was boots, and his first hat was a cowboy hat. He would stand on his big, high front porch and practice tipping his hat and thanking the crowd for his win. He was a cowboy. Every day, he would ride out with his parents to check on the cattle in the pastures around their big ranch.

When he was six years old, he got his first horse. She was two years old, and they had plans to grow up together. Her name was Sugar, and that was perfect, as she was the sweetest thing he had ever received. His sister's horse was named Lollipop, and so on their farm there were a lot of sweet things. For example, in the early morning, they had to go out before school and give the horses sweet feed.

Now, Cole had a contagious smile as big as Texas. He loved everybody he met and never met a stranger. He attended a cowboy church nearby when they were not on the road heading to a rodeo. It was there he met his best friend Jesus. Cole realized at a young age that he wanted to go to heaven when he died. He knew riding horses was sometimes dangerous and accidents could happen. So one Sunday morning, he trusted Jesus as his Savior. This gave him assurance that if one day he died, he would be riding with Jesus.

He was so sure of what he believed that one day at a bus stop, he passed out some plastic bracelets to his friends about Jesus. He even told one of the kids, "If anything ever happens to me, give one of these to my best friend. You just never know, especially when you ride horses as I do, what might happen." He loved horses, and just the smell of living on that ranch brought joy to his sweet, kind soul.

The day came when Cole started learning how to ride more and more. Sugar and he would spend hours riding around the pasture. As he trotted around the ranch, he would talk to God about things. He was a thankful kind of kid and would even sing songs he had learned about God. He was good on his horse, and it seemed even Sugar loved spending her time with Cole. Eventually, he and Sugar got so good that they were able to win the all-around champion title in a competition.

Cole had another dream, and that was to one day become a doctor. Cole loved people, and he had purpose in his heart to help people from a young age. If someone was hurt, he was the first one there to give help or comfort. So that meant in school, he had to study hard. His teachers said he gave 110 percent to everything he accomplished. Once as Cole was talking to himself at school, his teacher bent down and asked him whom he was talking to. He smiled with that big Texas grin and quietly said, "Jesus."

One day when Cole was out riding, he had an accident and took a fall. It scared him and his parents really badly, but after a while, he was back on Sugar, "riding with Jesus," as he would say. Jesus was his best friend, and they would take off into the sunset together.

Then there came the day for his first real rodeo run. He too was learning to barrel race like his sister. He was also learning to calf rope and was becoming very good at it. So now when his parents packed up on weekends, they had two powerful, beautiful, and sweet horses to raring go. Sugar and Lollipop were off to win at the rodeo. And they did win many a buckle.

At a rodeo one weekend, Cole met a clown by the name of Sandy. She had big overalls on, red hair, and a big sack of candy. She too had a big smile. Sandy the clown had balloons of all colors, and she also had something special in her bag besides candy.

Sandy the clown had some little books about Jesus. Cole loved it when he read one, and he followed Sandy around that day for a while before his event. She too shared Cole's love for Jesus, and she came to the rodeo to share that with all the kids there.

Years passed, and Cole became more and more of a rodeo professional. All though high school, he rode instead of playing sports. He chose to ride as many weekends as he could, but he still had his dream of becoming a doctor one day. His life was very busy doing things he loved.

One thing Cole learned about having Sugar was the responsibility of taking care of something other than himself. He took great care getting up on cold, blustery mornings to feed Sugar and heading off to school. Even in the summer, he did not mind getting up early to feed her, especially since his Mom and Dad always had a great breakfast cooking and the smell of bacon and hot biscuits made life even better.

Cole was winning many gold buckles in the big rodeos and attending college at the same time. He had to make a hard decision. It was time to hang up his hat and pursue his other life goal of becoming a doctor. It was getting hard to ride weekends and keep up with his college studies. But oh, how Cowboy Cole loved his rodeo life.

One weekend, while he was riding saddle bronc in a PRCA (Professional Rodeo Cowboy Association) rodeo event, something truly bad happened. He had been warned the horse he was going to ride bareback that day was going to be a challenge. This horse was known for hurting many cowboys. Cole was in the chute ready to take him on, and even there the horse was wild, trying to buck him off. He prayed, "Oh, Jesus, help me not to get hurt."

As Cole held on tight, he sensed that this was not going to be good. The chute opened, the crowd was cheering, and the horse was determined to throw Cole off. He did, and Cole hit the ground hard, so hard he passed out for a few moments. The crowd stopped cheering and fell silent, waiting to see if Cole was going to get up. After a few moments, Cole came around and stood up, looking for his hat and dusting off the dirt.

The crowd went wild for Cole. As he tipped his hat at the crowd and walked off, he knew in his heart that was his last big rodeo ride. He realized that day that God had a bigger-than-rodeo plan for his life. He smiled and looked up at Jesus, knowing that the next ride would be difficult also. Cole was ready for that challenge, and there was not much that scared Cole as long as Jesus was with him to the end.

Cole continued his studies and became a doctor. He never lost his love for horses and the rodeo. Sugar was still on his parents' ranch, so he could see her when he visited, and that he did often. *The cowboy life is the best way to grow up,* he thought to himself, *especially when you are riding with Jesus.*

What's About a Ball?

Throw me the ball! Kick it to the goal! Get a hole in one! Hit it out of the park! Touchdown! Hit it over the net! Slam dunk! Go team! There are so many sports we all love to play and so many teams formed to work together and win. This is nothing new to our God. Throughout the Bible, teams were working together to win.

What's about a ball? It is round, much like the world, which is spinning and revolving on its axis. And teams? Well, that's nothing new. Throughout the Bible, there were some great teams, and everybody on these teams had some different personalities that lead to victories.

Jesus picked a special twelve for His miracle team. They all had different skills and strengths. They had the best coach in the world: Coach Jesus, who was God in the flesh and knew everything about them. He knew their strengths and their weaknesses. He had a plan for each one of them on the team and a purpose to win the greatest victory for all eternity.

His training camp would be tough, but He knew, with discipline and the love of Coach Jesus, that they would have the victory in the end. A miracle team with the everlasting prize of heaven.

He even knew the one that would be benched and would not be in the miracle team. Coach Jesus allowed him to be on the team anyway. He wanted him to have a chance, as Coach Jesus always has hope for all His team players. No coach would love his team more than Coach Jesus. He would even give His life for this team.

Peter was one of the chosen to be on the miracle team. He was an aggressive guy and was ready for the challenge. He was full of fire, and at times he would say and do things without thinking. But when he failed Coach Jesus three times, he had enough of himself, and he turned his thinking around. Peter got on fire for the team and the eternal victory that was ahead. He never turned his back on the coach or his team again. It was said that Peter became great at getting the team where they needed to be on the playing field. His fire and zeal, when tamed by Coach Jesus, were said by Coach to be the rock of the team. "And I tell you are Peter, and on this Rock I will build my church" (Matthew 16:18).

Is this you? (Or if a girl teammate, Phoebe.)

Andrew was so excited about his new coach Jesus that he brought Peter even to meet Him. Andrew was friendly and probably the most excited about the forming of this new team. He sensed there was something great about his coach Jesus, as he knew there was victory ahead. They could and would be the miracle team. He saw Coach Jesus take five fishes and two loaves of bread and feed thousands. He never thought for a moment about the victories this team would have with the miracle coach Jesus leading them. He was an organizer, and this would be his place on the team. Looking ahead at what the team needed was his focus. Andrew did not have to be visible but knew that playing the backfield was as important as any other position on this victory team.

Is this you? (Or if a girl teammate, Ashleigh.)

James the Great, as he was called, was one of the bolder ones on the team. James stopped his profession and believed right from the beginning. He was so bold and excited about his new coach Jesus that he followed Him immediately. Not holding back anything, he left all and joined the miracle team. His nickname was "Son of Thunder," and that he was. I can see James running ahead just filled with excitement, giving everybody high fives. When he played on this team, it was as if lighting was in the air. He knew the true power of Coach Jesus and even asked the coach one time if He wanted him to take out their enemies by fire. Coach Jesus said, "No, we need to be kind and let them see what our team is truly about."

Is this you? (Or if a girl teammate, Jaclyn.)

John was loved much by Coach Jesus. He was "the disciple whom Jesus loved" (John 13:23). John was also known to love others. He was probably the youngest on the team and needed lots of attention from his coach, and he got it. He became an evangelist for the team. He was always telling people about the mission of the team and the eternal victory they would have in the end. They would win the biggest prize of all: eternal life for all who believe. Love would win, as the team would see how Coach Jesus Christ laid down His life not only for them, but also for the whole world. John did a lot of travel with and for the team. He never pointed others to himself, but always pointed them to the victory. He truly had infectious love, and when the morale was down, John the Beloved was there to encourage the team with his contagious love and smile.

Is this you? (Or a girl teammate, Jeanne.)

Philip was the quiet one on the team. He was strong and had a matter of "facts" about him. He analyzed things. He did not talk much to Coach Jesus but was a great learner. Philip wanted to make sure throughout his life that the team was following the rulebook. He even had a conversation with Coach Jesus about the commandments (or rules) and keeping them. "Whoever has my commands and obeys them, he is the one who loves me" (John 14:21). He wanted to win the right way and not cheat at anything. Philip had wisdom, and his name meant "lover of horses." He must have been strong in stature and would have made a great lineman, guard, or goalie on the team.

Is this you? (Or a girl teammate named Phyllis.)

Then there was Bartholomew, who had a nickname of Nathaniel. Peter, his close friend, introduced him to Coach Jesus. His nickname, Nathaniel, meant "gift of God." He must have been something special for someone to have given him that name. He was the suspicious one who asked about Coach, "Can any good thing (person) come from Nazareth?" which was Coach Jesus's hometown. His teammate Philip replied, "Come and see." And he did, and he joined the miracle team. Even after all was done to his coach, he was one of those present when Coach Jesus ascended back into heaven, His home. Nathaniel was very honest and spoke his mind about things. Coach Jesus liked that about him. Nathaniel was honest and wanted everyone to play fair on the team.

Is this you? (Or a girl teammate, Natasha.)

Matthew was the well-educated teammate. He came from a wealthy home. He loved money and did things that were not so right in collecting people's taxes. His social skills were not the best, and he was not well liked for his profession. But Coach Jesus saw something within him that he wanted to change. And Matthew did change when he saw a hope for himself in doing something on the miracle team. Doing something good was within his heart, but only Coach Jesus could teach him in training camp. Matthew wanted to change, and he did. He now had a new purpose to help others, not cheat them. Matthew's pride turned to humility. He did not care what others thought, and that pushed him to the goal and the victory ahead.

Is this you? (Or a girl teammate, Mattie.)

Jude was a skilled fisherman. So for him to leave his trade join this team was life changing. He himself was a leader of fishermen and wanted to follow someone who would make the world a place where things were better. Fishing was a difficult profession, and little did he know that his new life with the miracle team would be even harder. The eternal rewards of the miracle team would outweigh any amount of fish or food he could provide for his family and others. He was young, had good health, and gave up what he had to follow and learn a new way from Coach Jesus. He was aggressive on the team and brought determination with goals set in his mind for the victories and hard work that were ahead.

Is this you? (Or girl teammate, Jordan.)

Thomas was known as one that doubted, and he came to the team with reservations about their goals and the truth of the purpose of the miracle team. He had to be convinced that his coach was the real deal and would lead them to the eternal victory. He had been waiting for this team and Coach Jesus, but he just wanted to test things before giving his life for the victory. He knew that playing on this team would and could be dangerous, as the opposing side was vicious and would stop at nothing to kill the teammates. He, like some of us, wanted to see and touch the real thing. When Coach Jesus died for the team and the final victory was won, Thomas wanted to touch and see the wounds received by Coach Jesus, who died for the sins of the world, including Thomas. After this, he believed and was no longer a skeptic. He went to work for the miracle team immediately and encouraged more teams called churches to be formed. His goal was then to preach about his Jesus and build churches (teams) for the glory of God.

Is this you? (Or girl teammate, Theresa.)

James the Less was called by Coach Jesus to be on the team and became a devout team player. He had a burden to do what was right, to the point that he ate no meat and only vegetables. He wanted his physical body to be the best. He focused so much on the miracle team and the eternal victory that his knees were calloused after spending so much time in prayer. James knew the enemy would be great, and that to win, they needed power from God the Creator above. It was recorded in history that when he took a beating for the team for telling the game plan, the Pharisees threw him from the pinnacle (or top floor) of the temple he landed on his feet. He was in great physical shape for the miracle team. He was strong, courageous, and determined to win.

Is this you? (Or a girl Jasmine?)

Then there was Simon the Zealot. Just the word *zealot* describes this teammate Coach Jesus picked. A zealot is someone who is a fanatic, like a fan out of control at a football game or other sporting event. He knew his team was the only one that mattered and his views were right, no matter what anyone else thought.

He was a fighter on the team and would probably be the one to start a fight when someone hurt or disagreed with the coach. He had to be tamed to be successful. Simon the Zealot had to trade his sword of fighting for the cross of Christ. The same zeal he had was transferred to the miracle team's victories. He became the one known as the enthusiastic evangelist, spreading the good news of the victory of Jesus the Messiah whom he and others had been waiting for.

Is this you? (Or a girl, Simone.)

Judas was asked to be on the team also. The heart of Judas was his problem. He wanted fame and fortune, like some team players are seeking today. He was not a team player but a man consumed with his own desires. It was all about him and what he could get out of it. He wanted the fortune he could gain from the team and Coach Jesus. He asked the carry the purse, and slowly, his greed consumed him. Some team players, even today, are not there for the victory of the team but for their own selfish desires. Judas, after betraying Jesus and his team, hanged himself. His own desires destroyed him, but not the team. They went on without him and replaced him, possibly with Paul, the greatest team player of all.

Is this you? (Or a girl, Jodie.)

The victory of the miracle team, with Jesus as our coach, still goes on today. Every person playing on any team is one of these above. Great strength is required for the victories. And some are learning how to overcome their own weaknesses for the victory of winning as a team. Teamwork shows unity and finding your place to make others successful as you play the game. We are all in this journey of life together. Maybe you are not the one scoring all the points, but you are there making the score possible by using your strengths for the ultimate win of the team.

So is the body of Christ. For those of us who know Jesus Christ as our Lord and Savior, the team we are on wins the eternal victory.

These men knew that Jesus was the coach of their lives. His example took them to the task, and as He went before them, they knew it would be worth even their deaths to follow Him and to give everything they had for His cause and the purpose of the victory.

Why Can't I Have That?

When I was a child, there was something I truly wanted. I had made several requests, but it seemed when I mentioned it to my parents, they just ignored me. It would be on my Christmas wish list or my birthday list, and that wish was just ignored. I thought, *Well, maybe it's too expensive.* I came from a home where hard work was my dad's life. I just could not let it go. It must cost too much money or they would get if for me—so I thought.

Some of the girls and boys at school had them around their necks. Some were made of gold or silver and were very shiny, and one I really liked had a diamond in the middle. It was so beautiful, I thought. I wanted one like that so badly. I have always loved shiny things.

Then there were the kind where Jesus was still on it. I did not care for that one in particular because I knew Jesus had died hanging naked, and they had Him covered up around His waist. He did have a crown of thorns on His head.

But He did not look all wounded and bleeding, like I had pictured from what I had read in the Bible. The one where two pieces of splintered wood were put together and they laid Him down and nailed Him to that. Then they lifted it off the ground, and then He hung there until He died.

Yes, I am talking about a cross necklace that I so wanted to wear around my neck. After my persistence, my gracious father finally told me his answer. I had never thought about what he told me, but I always wanted to know, "Why?" As a kid, I had so many questions, and I think it drove my parents a little crazy at times. "Why this? Why that?" I would always ask.

When my dad spoke, I listened, and this is what he finally said about wearing a cross necklace: "Why would you want that remembrance around your neck? It is not something to be looked upon as beautiful. His death was not gold, silver, or pretty. It was a disgrace for Jesus the Son of God to hang there with a broken body. The cross was a curse for the people that died there." My dad said, "I do not want you to think about the suffering He did for our sins, but some people that wear them do not realize that Christ paid for our sins and it's done. Jesus Christ does not want us to think and dwell on that. He wants us to think of Him as a risen Savior and live the new life He created for those who believe. He is alive and done with paying for our sins! Someone had to pay, and that someone was Jesus Christ the Lord. The cross was disgraceful, but it was the way Jesus wanted us to see how painful and shameful sin is. He took our sins on Himself; it was the way He chose to do it. Jesus Himself said, 'It is finished,'" My dad concluded, and with that, I never asked my parents for a cross to wear around my neck again.

Even now, as I have been given beautiful cross necklaces. I find it so difficult to wear them. For my heart is grieved when I think about the painful, shameful death Jesus died for me. I know He came and experienced all of life so He could feel what we feel and have pity on us. So maybe in choosing this kind of death, He could show us the pain and shame that comes from our sins!

So you see, someone did pay, and it's Jesus. So the next time you see someone wearing a cross, do not look at that person and judge, but say as I do now: "I am thankful for the cross that Jesus died on for me, but I am so glad He is alive!"

I will never understand that kind of love. "For God demonstrates His love toward us in that while we were yet sinners. Christ died for us!" (Romans 5:8).

That year on my birthday, my dad bought me a necklace to

wear. It was a silver heart with a very tiny diamond it. He said in the card, "The heart of Jesus was love, and His love shines like a diamond." And with that, I knew why my daddy did not want me to wear a cross.